W9-AHF-464

EVERYDAY GUIDES
MADE EASY

Google
Apps

Publisher's note: Official UK and US prices are given, displayed as '£xx/$xx', rather than a conversion based on the exchange rate.

Publisher and Creative Director: Nick Wells
Project Editor: Polly Prior
Art Director: Mike Spender
Layout Design: Jane Ashley
Digital Design and Production: Chris Herbert
Screenshots: Luke Johnson
Copy Editor: Anna Groves
Technical Editor: Mark Mayne
Proofreader: Dawn Laker
Indexer: Eileen Cox

Special thanks to: Catherine Taylor

This edition first published 2017 by
FLAME TREE PUBLISHING
6 Melbray Mews
Fulham, London SW6 3NS
United Kingdom

www.flametreepublishing.com

© 2017 Flame Tree Publishing

ISBN 978-1-78664-197-7

A CIP record for this book is available from the British Library upon request.

Printed in China.

All non-screenshot pictures are courtesy of Shutterstock.com and © the following photographers:1 ESB Professional; 3 Anmet Misirligul; 5 Benny Marty; 6 AstroStar; 7 kikujungboy; 8 dennizn; 14 ESB Professional; 22 Sergey Nivens; 25, 90 everything possible; 29 dennizn; 31 NIRUT RUPKHAM; 48 Rawpixel.com; 66 Indypendenz; 78 Eugenio Marongiu; 82 Pixelagestudio; 87 g-stockstudio; 96 pikcha; 100 vectorfusionart; 106 PureSolution; 110 Twin Design; 122 Antonio Guillem; 123 fizkes; 124 Robert Lucian Crusitu; 125 style-photography.

EVERYDAY GUIDES
MADE EASY

Google
Apps

LUKE JOHNSON

FOREWORD BY MARK MAYNE

FLAME TREE
PUBLISHING

CONTENTS

Never used Google apps before? This chapter explains
exactly what they are and how you can get started.

Here we explore and explain Google Drive, the home of the
Google apps, and how you can access it on all your devices.

It's time to communicate better. This chapter looks at Gmail
and Calendar, and what you need to know about using them.

Here we look at Google Docs and Sheets, and how
you can work with others thanks to the cloud.

For budding business users, this chapter will teach you how to
make presentations and websites using Slides and Sites.

Now you've mastered the basics, this chapter will guide you through
the next step of Google's apps, including Google+ and Vault.

FOREWORD

When computers were growing up and dinosaurs roamed the earth, simple word processing, presentation creation or spreadsheet editing meant installing and running software on your machine. If you swapped computers, you'd need to physically carry any files across (floppy disk anyone?), and hope the new software was compatible with your previous computer's install. Files often corrupted, computers crashed and wiped recent work, and simply forgetting to copy across a document could easily mean wasted hours.

However, way back in 2007, Google decided to put a stop to all this nonsense, and launched Google Docs, which has evolved over a decade into Google Apps, or latterly G Suite. It took the desktop 'office' software of yore and simply hosted it in the cloud, thus providing all the general office tools you would want, but through your browser or via specific Apple and Android apps. The result is that your business or life organization tools are at your fingertips wherever you are, and on whatever device you choose.

This changed everything, and although the suite of tools has expanded over the years, it still fulfils the same niche. Once you've tried it, you'll never have it any other way!

This guide takes you from the first principles of what G Suite is, how to access it and simple tasks to complete once you have created an account, through to more advanced operations as you grow in confidence.

From managing your calendar appointments, creating to-do items, accessing existing documents and creating new ones, through to collaborating with groups of people in real time, chat and audio calling, and livestreaming, G Suite can help you, and already does for millions of people every day. Come and join them!

Mark Mayne, Mayne Media Ltd

INTRODUCTION

This guide tells you everything you need to know to get started with Google apps. From the very basics to more advanced tools, *Everyday Guides Made Easy: Google Apps* will help you through it all.

YOUR GUIDE TO GOOGLE APPS

Google is more than a search engine. Google apps are changing the way people do things, both professionally and personally. They allow you to collaborate in teams on single documents and let you access all your files, no matter where in the world you are, or what machine you're using.

GETTING INVOLVED

This book has been designed to help you find your way through the world of Google apps. It will teach you to create documents that friends and colleagues can work on, and even help you produce your first website. Getting started with Google apps can feel daunting, but once you've mastered the basics, you'll never look back.

Hot Tips

Look out for Hot Tips throughout this book. These quick, digestible points provide special insight into how to get the most out of key Google apps features. They will highlight shortcuts and introduce time saving techniques.

STEP-BY-STEP GUIDES

This book has been designed to provide a useful, easy-to-follow resource for those new to Google apps. Each section will offer step-by-step guides to walk you through a number of Google apps, including Google Docs, Google Sheets and Gmail.

EASY EXPLANATIONS

Forget the technical terms and unnecessarily complicated jargon. Wherever possible, we've cut through the fluff to bring you a simple, easy-to-understand guide. Helping walk you through some of the more complicated processes, step-by-step guides will highlight the exact actions you need to take in order to accomplish certain tasks, and annotated images will explain what each button does.

WHAT ARE GOOGLE APPS?

ONLINE APPS

Want an easier way to work? Google apps are the answer. A collection of online software tools that let you do create anything from text documents and spreadsheets to presentations and websites, they are the modern answer to Microsoft Office. Instead of being installed directly on your machine, however, they live online and can be accessed through the internet. Here we'll look at what exactly Google apps are, and how you can start using them.

WHERE CAN YOU USE GOOGLE APPS?

As they are stored on the web, Google apps let you access and update your files from anywhere in the world. Any computer, smartphone or tablet that's connected to the internet can be used to access your files.

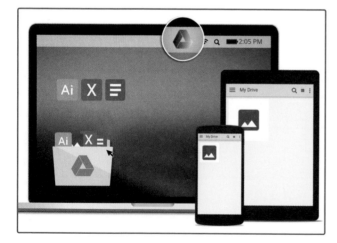

Above: Google apps are stored on the web and can be accessed from any of your connected devices.

WHO CAN SEE MY DOCUMENTS?

Despite not being stored on your machine, your Google apps files can only be seen by you, so don't worry. You'll need a username and password to access them. If you want, however, you can invite others to see and even edit certain documents in real time. Colleagues given permission to view a file will only be able to view that one. All of your other documents will remain private.

HOW MUCH DO GOOGLE APPS COST?

You can use all the Google apps for free on a personal basis – all you need is a free Google account. If, however, you want to use them for your business, you can pay a monthly fee to gain access to the added features offered by G Suite, Google's premium service. G Suite prices start at £3.30/$5 per user per month and rise to £6.60/$10 per user per month. The more you pay, the more features you get.

WHAT IS G SUITE?

G Suite is made of the same Google apps as the free model – Docs, Sheets, Slides, etc. – with additional services, such as Google Vault, thrown in. G Suite can also sync across a number of users, making it ideal for business use. On top of this, G Suite lets you use Gmail as an email host while adding your own custom address such as Dave@DaveDesigns.com.

Above: G Suite is for business users and, among other things, lets you create your own email addresses.

THE BENEFITS OF USING GOOGLE APPS

Why should you use Google apps over traditional software? There are many reasons, ranging from cost to ease of use. Compared with traditional software packages like Microsoft Office, Google apps have so much more to offer.

IT'S FREE

If you're a personal user, you can make use of everything from email and calendars to document makers and photo storage without spending a penny.

YOU CAN WORK REMOTELY

As they are all stored online, Google apps can be accessed from nearly anywhere in the world. All you need is an internet connection.

YOU CAN SHARE THE WORKLOAD

Being based online lets you share documents with friends and colleagues. You can let them view content or update it, and watch in real time as updates are being made.

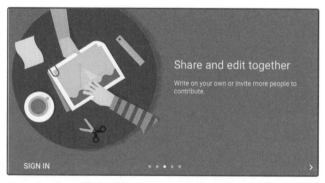

Share and edit together

Write on your own or invite more people to contribute.

SIGN IN

Above: Google apps allow multiple users to share documents and edit them simultaneously from different devices.

ACCESS FOR MOBILE

You're not locked to working on your desktop or laptop. Free-to-download smartphone and tablet apps are available for both iOS and Android users.

DON'T WORRY ABOUT UPDATES

Another benefit of online apps is that there are no software updates to slow you down. All program updates automatically run in the background. That means no more annoying pop-ups.

SAVES ARE AUTOMATIC

You can no longer accidentally close a document without saving it. Google automatically saves all your files as you work.

HOT-DESKING OPTIONS

If you're a business user, Google apps make hot-desking possible. As documents are stored online, rather than on a specific machine, staff can sit at any work terminal.

Automatically save to the web

Never lose your progress, so you can keep working from any computer or device.

SIGN IN

Above: There's no need to press a button or worry about lost files, Google apps save your progress as you type.

BUT BEAR IN MIND...

Of course, the payoff for these brilliant free tools is that Google gains a certain amount of access to your data, so it's worth checking out Google's detailed privacy policies (at www.google.co.uk/intl/en/policies/privacy) to make sure you're happy with that.

INTRODUCING CLOUD COMPUTING

Google apps aren't stored directly on your machine. Instead, they are based on the internet, on something called 'the cloud'. You might have heard it talked about, but what exactly is the cloud?

WHAT IS CLOUD COMPUTING?

The cloud isn't a single, physical thing. Instead, cloud computing is the process of storing information, documents and programs on a series of interconnected servers. Servers can perform different functions, such as remotely storing information or managing access to a centralized resource.

HOW DOES THE CLOUD WORK?

By connecting all of these servers, the cloud lets you access your files wherever you are. One server might host all your individual files, while another delivers the software used to make Google apps work. Joining on the internet, though, they bring everything together instantly wherever you want to work.

ACCESSING GOOGLE APPS

Now you know a little bit more about Google apps, it's time to start playing with them. This is how you get started.

APPS WORKING TOGETHER

Google apps are about multiple apps working seamlessly together. No matter which app you're in, you're only ever two clicks away from jumping to another service.

WHAT DEVICES CAN YOU USE TO ACCESS THEM?

Given that they are based online rather than locked to a single machine, you can use almost any device to access Google apps. We're not just talking about your desktop or laptop either. Thanks to a range of Google-made iPhone- and Android-friendly mobile applications, you can access them on your smartphone or tablet too.

Above: Google apps can be downloaded to your iOS or Android smartphone for free.

Google Apps on Android Phones

If you've got an Android phone, you should have some Google apps such as Google Docs and Google Drive pre-installed. If not, don't worry; you can download them all for free simply by visiting the Google Play Store.

Downloading Google Apps for iPhone

Google and Apple might not be friends, but they support many of each other's services. As such, you can fill your iPhone or iPad with Google apps and enjoy the likes of Google Docs, Sheets and Gmail on the move. How? On your iPhone or iPad, follow these simple steps:

○ **Open the App Store:** This is the blue icon with the white letter 'A' in a white circle.

○ **Select 'Search':** This can be found on the menu at the bottom of the screen.

○ **Enter search term:** Type in the app you're looking for – e.g. Google Docs, Google Search, etc. – and hit enter.

○ **Download:** Click 'Get' to download the free app.

IS YOUR BROWSER SUPPORTED?

Google apps work with the two most recent versions of the world's four most popular internet browsers: Chrome, Firefox, Microsoft Edge and Safari. Although the apps work with other browsers, including Opera, some features might be missing.

USING GOOGLE APPS OFFLINE

Just because they're stored on the web doesn't mean Google apps have to stay there. The Google Docs Offline extension (available in the Chrome browser only) can be downloaded to your computer, letting you access files away from the internet. The changes are then synced to the cloud when you re-connect.

Above: Although stored on the internet, you can download your files and access them when disconnected from the web.

WHAT CAN I DO?

From creating documents to managing your emails, Google apps are here to make your life easier. There are features for all levels of users. Here are just a few examples.

SEND EMAIL

Creating a Google account gives you a Gmail email address. Gmail is the most popular email client in the world.

STORE YOUR PHOTOS

Through Google Drive you can store all of your photos in one place and access them on any device around the world.

CREATE DOCUMENTS AND PRESENTATIONS

Docs is Google's answer to Microsoft Word and lets you create text documents, while Sheets and Slides make spreadsheets and presentations respectively.

KEEP TRACK OF YOUR CALENDAR

An online calendar means you can check your upcoming appointments wherever you are.

STAY IN TOUCH WITH FRIENDS

Google Hangouts lets you message and share images with friends for free. Cheaper than texting, it's similar to WhatsApp or Facebook Messenger.

Above: A calendar app lets you manage your schedule anywhere in the world.

YOUR ACCOUNT

Before you can use any of the Google apps, you'll need to create a Google account. This is free and easy to do, and comes with a new Google email address.

THE DIFFERENT ACCOUNTS

There are three types of account you can use. The first, which is automatically created simply by setting up a Gmail email address, is completely free. You can also pay for two types of G Suite account. These cost £3.30/$5 or £6.60/$10 per user per month and give you improved multi-user collaboration and additional services.

Which Google Package Is Best for Me?

For personal and small business use, a standard Google account will be fine. You'll only need a G Suite account if you're running a business with multiple users.

> **Hot Tip**
>
> Unsure which account is right for you? You can try out G Suite for free for 14 days.

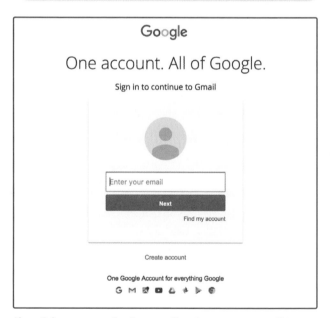

Above: Before you can use Google apps, you'll need to create an account. This is completely free.

CREATING YOUR GOOGLE ACCOUNT

A single Google account will allow you to use all of Google's apps, including Gmail, Google+, Google Maps and YouTube.

WHAT YOU NEED

To create your new Google account, you'll need the following information:

- Your full name.
- Your date of birth.
- Gender.
- Phone number.
- Current email address.

Why Does Google Need This?

If you're worried about your privacy, Google uses this information to authorize permission if in the future you forget your login information.

GETTING SET UP

Armed with the above information, you just need to follow these simple steps:

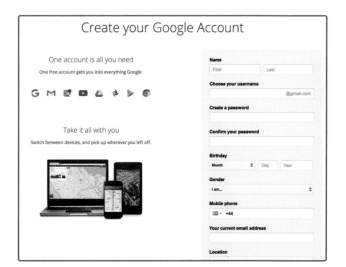

Above: Creating an account requires you to enter a range of personal details.

1. Visit www.gmail.com on your computer.

2. Click the large 'Create account' button.

3. Enter your personal details.

4. Choose your username. This will be your email address,
    so for example 'lukejohnsontest' would give you the
    email address lukejohnsontest@gmail.com. If your
    chosen username is already taken, Google will prompt
    you to select another.

5. Choose your password, which must be at least eight
    characters in length.

6. Click the 'Next step' button.

Hot Tip

Take your time and think carefully before selecting your Google username. Once set, you can't change it without creating a new email address.

What Next?

You're well on your way to
having a Google account, but
first you need to read through
Google's terms and conditions
before selecting the 'I agree'
option. Once you've agreed,
Google will send you a text
message with a code to verify
your information. Enter this
and that's it, congratulations,
you just created your own
Google account.

Privacy and Terms

By choosing "I agree" below you agree to Google's Terms of Service.

You also agree to our Privacy Policy, which describes how we process
your information, including these key points:

Data we process when you use Google

- When you use Google services to do things like write a message in Gmail
  or comment on a YouTube video, we store the information you create.

- When you search for a restaurant on Google Maps or watch a video on
  YouTube, for example, we process information about that activity –
  including information like the video you watched, device IDs, IP addresses,
  cookie data, and location.

- We also process the kinds of information described above when you use
  apps or sites that use Google services like ads, Analytics, and the YouTube
  video player.

CANCEL   I AGREE

Above: You'll have to agree to Google's Ts & Cs to create an account.

SIGNING IN

Once you've created your account, you'll be able to sign in whenever you like. To do this you'll need your username and password. Once signed in, you'll be able to access all of the Google apps.

SIGNING OUT

On any Google apps page your email address or profile picture will show in the top-right corner. Clicking this gives you the opportunity to sign out. You should do this after every login on a machine used by other people.

CAN YOU HAVE MULTIPLE ACCOUNTS?

Absolutely. Google will let you sign up for as many accounts as you want. Each one will create a new email address and store your created documents separately. Many people have both personal and professional accounts.

GETTING A BUSINESS ACCOUNT

If you decide you want a business account, you can sign up to G Suite by visiting gsuite.google.com, clicking 'Get started now' and following the set-up process.

G Suite by Google Cloud

Home   Products ▾   Pricing   Learning ▾   Support   Sign in

CONTACT US   GET STARTED

Choose your G Suite plan. The first 14 days are free.

BEST VALUE

Basic
Professional office suite with 30GB storage

$5
per user per month

GET STARTED

Business
Enhanced office suite with unlimited storage and archiving

$10
per user per month

GET STARTED

✓ Business email through Gmail
✓ Video and voice conferencing
✓ Smart shared calendars

✓ Business email through Gmail
✓ Video and voice conferencing
✓ Smart shared calendars

Above: Business accounts with additional features can be created, but they'll cost you.

A safe place fo

Go to Goo

all your files

ive

STORE, SHARE AND SYNC

INTRODUCING GOOGLE DRIVE

Google Drive is the homepage for all of your content. It's where all your files from all the Google apps are stored. You can also access each of the individual apps from this central hub.

HOW MUCH STORAGE DO YOU GET?

The amount of Google Drive storage available to you depends on whether you're willing to pay, and if so, how much.

The Free Allowance

Every Google account holder gets 15GB of data completely free. That's enough to store around 5,000 photos.

Additional Storage

If you need it, you can buy more space. Upgrading to 100GB of cloud storage (around 33,000 photos) will cost £1.59/$1.99 per month. You can also select a massive 1TB of storage (more than 330,000 photos), but this will cost £7.99/$9.99 per month.

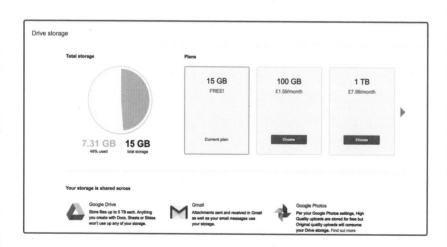

Left: All Google accounts include 15GB of free storage but you can pay for more if needed.

ACCESSING GOOGLE DRIVE

As well as letting you access all of your files, Google Drive gives you access to your documents wherever and whenever you like. That's because it can be used on multiple devices simultaneously. Assuming you're logged in and have an internet connection, that is. If you've stayed signed in on your work computer, you can still look at your files on your laptop at home that night.

Google Drive on Mobile

As well as being accessible via your laptop's or desktop's internet browser, Google Drive can be used on your smartphone and tablet. You can log in using your portable device's browser, but there is an easier option – the Google Drive app.

Downloading the App

If you run an Android phone or tablet, the Google Drive app will already be pre-installed. Go on, take a look. If, however, you're an iPhone and iPad user, you'll need to download it. Don't worry, it's easy and free. Just search the App Store for Google Drive and press 'Get'.

Above: As well as being accessible on your computer, you can download a Google Drive smartphone app.

WHAT CAN I STORE ON GOOGLE DRIVE?

Google Drive lets you store all of your emails, attachments, documents and photos. Everything you create using Google apps are stored on Google Drive. You can also add and upload other, non-Google files from your devices to it.

BACKING UP IMAGES

If you add Google Drive to your phone, you can set your photos to backup into your Drive account. This means if your phone is ever lost or stolen, you will still have a copy of your snaps stored remotely. You can choose to store original images or compress them to a high quality to store more at once.

Buying More Storage

To buy more storage, you can click the 'Upgrade storage' option within your Google Drive. This is in the left-hand menu panel. Clicking it will give you a number of new storage options.

Right: Google Drive lets you store all of your photos from all of your devices in one place.

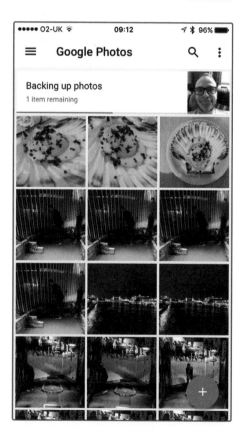

THE GOOGLE DRIVE HOMEPAGE ON DESKTOP

Every time you log in to your Google Drive, this is the page you'll see. It's the homepage to your Google apps experience; here is what all the menus and buttons do.

1   New: Clicking this button opens a drop-down menu with shortcuts for creating new files within each of the core Google apps, folders and uploads.

2   My Drive: A shortcut back to the homepage of your personal Google Drive.

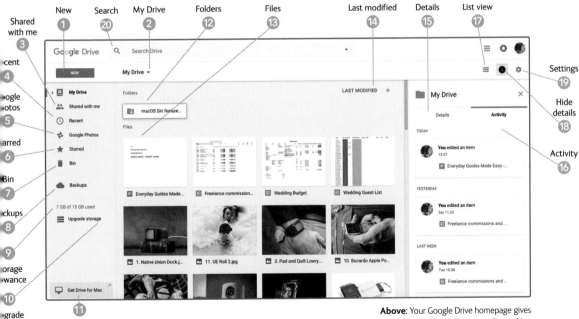

New   Search   My Drive   Folders   Files   Last modified   Details   List view

Shared with me   1   20   2   12   13   14   15   17

3   Settings   19

cent   4   Hide details   18

ogle otos   5   Activity   16

arred   6

Bin   7

ckups   8

9

orage wance   10

grade   11   **Above:** Your Google Drive homepage gives you access to all your files.

Get Drive for Mac

③ **Shared with me**: This shows only those files created by others and shared with you for viewing or editing.

④ **Recent**: Reorganizes all your files based on those you have most recently edited. Files are organized by days, weeks and months the further you go back.

Hot Tip

You can star any file by right-clicking it and selecting the 'Add star' option from the pop-up menu.

⑤ **Google Photos**: All of your photos and videos are stored here in a timeline of when they were shot.

⑥ **Starred**: Special storage for all of your most important files and documents.

⑦ **Bin**: Deleted items can be recovered from here.

⑧ **Backups**: You can track when your Android devices were last backed up here.

⑨ **Storage allowance**: How much of your storage allowance is remaining.

⑩ **Upgrade storage**: Click here to buy additional storage.

⑪ **Get Drive for Mac**: A shortcut to downloading Google's offline apps. If you're a PC user, you'll be offered a PC-friendly version.

⑫ **Folders**: All of your folders are stored under this tab.

⑬ **Files**: This is where all of your files from all Google apps are stored together.

⑭ **Last modified**: These are the documents and files you used most recently.

(15) Details: Here you can see information on highlighted files, including when they were created and the storage they're using.

(16) Activity: Here you can see a breakdown of all the times you've edited a selected file.

(17) List view: Clicking this will show all your files in a list rather than a grid.

(18) Hide details: Don't want that details sidebar? Clicking this button will remove it.

(19) Settings: Clicking this will open the settings menu, which offers more advanced features.

(20) Search: Entering keywords here will search all of your Drive-stored files.

THE GOOGLE DRIVE HOMEPAGE ON MOBILE

If you're accessing your Google Drive from a mobile app, you'll see a different view. This is what the smartphone app looks like and the buttons you should know about.

1 **Menu:** Tapping this menu button will launch a sidebar offering access to your shared, recent and starred documents as well as your photos and other options.

2 **Search:** Pressing the search button lets you type out keywords or search for documents by file type, such as text documents, PDFs and videos.

3 **View:** Clicking this button will toggle your files between grid and list views.

4 **Select:** Long-touching a folder or file icon enables you to select individual, multiple or all Google Drive files simultaneously.

5 **Folders:** All of your Drive folders can be found here.

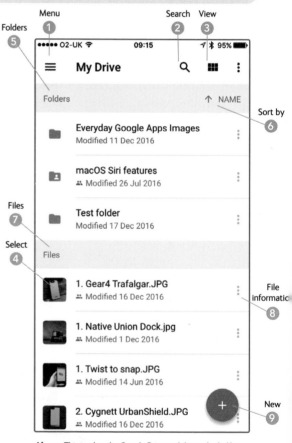

Above: This is what the Google Drive mobile app looks like.

Menu
Folders
Search View
Sort by **6**
Files **7**
Select **4**
File informatic **8**
New **9**

6 **Sort by:** Tapping this lets you change how your files are sorted and displayed. You can sort by name, last modified or storage used.

7 **Files:** This is where all of your individual files and documents are stored.

8 **File information:** Tap those three dots next to any file and you get a menu of options exclusive to that document. You can share it with people, move it, rename it or star it.

9 **New:** Tapping this big round plus symbol will give you a pop-up of creation options. You can create new files or folders, or launch your phone's camera to take a new photo.

Above: You can upload or create new documents direct from the app.

FILES AND FOLDERS

In this section we'll look at how you can create, upload and share files, and organize them within your own customized folders.

CREATING A NEW FILE

Possibly the most common task performed in Google apps, you can create a new file with just a couple of quick clicks. The process you need to follow depends on the type of file you're looking to create.

Creating a File from Drive

If you're in Google Drive, you'll need to select 'New' in the top-left corner of the screen

Above: To create a new Google Drive file or folder, you'll have to click the 'New' button.

and then click on 'Docs', 'Sheets' or 'Slides', depending on which you need, from the drop-down menu.

Creating a File from Apps

Amazingly, this is even easier. If you're already in Docs, Sheets or Slides, just click the large 'blank' document in the upper-left corner and a new file will be created.

UPLOADING A FILE

Just because a file wasn't originally created in Google apps doesn't mean it can't still live in your Google Drive, giving you access to it wherever you are. To upload a file to your Drive, you'll need to do the following:

1. Click 'New' on the Google Drive homepage.

2. Select 'File upload' from the drop-down menu.

3. Choose your desired file from your machine's folders and click 'Open'.

4. Your new file should now upload and appear in your Drive's file list.

Above: You can upload files to Drive direct from your computer.

Above: Google will alert you when your uploads are complete.

CREATING FOLDERS

Now you've started creating files, you're going to need folders to organize them and keep your Google Drive looking all neat and tidy. Fortunately, folders are easy to create, and there's no limit on the number you can have.

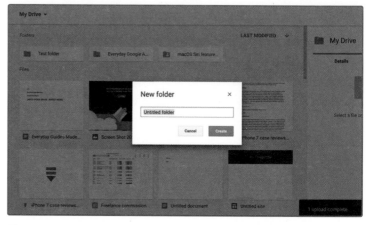

Above: Creating a new folder can be completed with just three clicks of your mouse.

How to Make a Folder

To create a folder for your Google Drive, you'll need to do the following:

1. Head to your Google Drive homepage.

2. Select the 'New' tab in the top-left corner of the page.

3. Select the 'Folder' option from the drop-down menu.

4. Give your new folder a name.

5. Select 'Create'.

Finding Your Folders

All of your folders sit at the top of your Google Drive, above individual files, making it easy to access your key documents. Now they're made, it's time to start filling these folders.

ORGANIZING FILES AND FOLDERS

With all these files and folders floating around, your Google Drive is going to start looking pretty busy. If you want to keep things organized, it's time to learn about moving, renaming and deleting files.

FILLING YOUR FOLDERS

Your folders can hold all the files, documents and images you want. How you move your file, however, will depend on where you're moving it from.

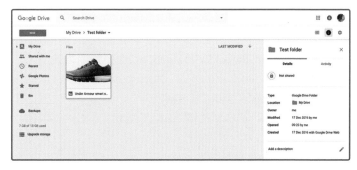

Above: You can fill your folders with whatever you like.

On Your Google Drive

If you're on the Google Drive homepage, the easiest way to move a file to a folder is to simply drag it. Click on the desired file once to select it, then pull it with your mouse or trackpad towards the folder you want to move it to. Releasing your mouse while the file is over the folder will see it dropped into the folder.

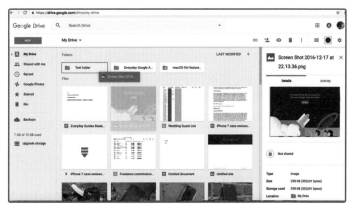

Above: Folders are listed at the top of your Google Drive homepage.

Within a File

If you're within a document and decide you want to move it to a certain folder, you'll need to do the following:

1. Click 'File' from the document's top row of menus.

2. Select 'Move to...' from the drop-down list.

3. In the pop-up window click 'Move this item'.

4. Click 'My Drive' from the list of options.

5. Select the folder you want to move the file to.

6. Press the 'Move' button.

Hot Tip

You can quickly move files into folders simply by dragging them and hovering over the desired folder, then releasing the mouse.

RENAMING FOLDERS

To give your folder a new name, you'll need to right-click on it and select the 'Rename' option from the drop-down menu. Once you've typed in your new name, hitting enter will rename the folder.

Above: You can rename your folder any time you like, making it easier to find.

COPYING FOLDERS

Want a duplicate? You can copy folders by downloading them to your machine or sharing them with another account. Both can be achieved by right-clicking the folder name in Drive.

SHARING YOUR FILES AND FOLDERS

Once you've created files and folders, you can start sharing them with friends and colleagues. This can make it easier to complete communal work projects, make plans with friends or let people view something you think they should see.

SHARING A FILE

You can share any file or photo on your Google Drive. To do this, you need to right-click on the file you want to share and select the 'Share' option from the pop-up window. Alternatively, you can click on the file and click the 'Share' icon that appears on the top menu.

With Whom?

The next step of sharing your file is selecting whom you're going to share it with. In the sharing window, you can enter the name of an existing contact, or the email address of someone new.

Clicking 'Send' will send an invitation to your chosen recipient. They will need to click the link in the email to view your file.

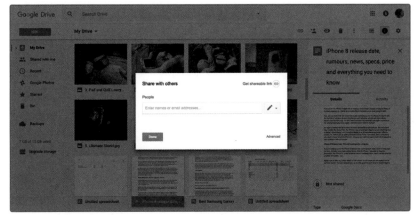

Right: You can share your folders with whomever you like just by entering their email address.

SHARING FOLDERS

It's not just individual files you can share. Whole folders can be shared by following the same process. Once shared, if you add more items to the folder, you'll be asked if you want these to be shared with those you've already shared your folder with.

SELECTING YOUR SHARING LIMITS

Before you share your files and folders, you have the option to choose how much access the recipient can enjoy. You can let people view your document, comment on it, or go one step further and give them full editing privileges.

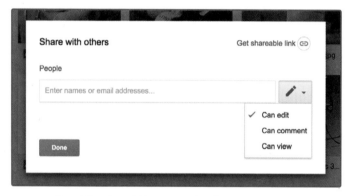

Above: When sharing folders, you can select if recipients can view, edit or comment on them.

Picking Your Limits

You can select the level of sharing you want to give people during the sharing process. When entering your contact's email address, click the down arrow by the pencil icon on the right. This gives you three options, letting recipients edit, comment or view.

LINK SHARING

It's not just your contacts you can share with. A feature called Link Sharing lets you generate a unique link that can be posted online or in an email thread. Anyone who then clicks this, whether you know them or not, can access that file.

> ## Hot Tip
>
> Creating a sharable link can let you share files with large friendship groups or an entire office without worrying about forgetting someone's email address.

Above: If you want your folder to be publicly available, you can create a link to share it widely.

Above: These links allow people to view, comment on or edit in the folder.

Types of Link Sharing

There are different levels of Link Sharing that set the amount of access people have. They include the following:

○ Anyone with the link can view.

○ Anyone with the link can comment.

○ Anyone with the link can edit.

ACCESSING YOUR FILES OFFLINE

Just because Google Drive files are stored in the cloud and accessed via the internet doesn't mean you can't access them offline too.

DOWNLOADING DRIVE

Clicking the 'Get Drive for Mac' or 'Get Drive for PC' buttons at the bottom of your Drive homepage will let you download an offline version of your Drive account. This will install software directly on to your machine, and create a new file on your computer's hard drive. By doing this, you can store your documents offline, letting you view and edit them without being connected to the internet.

Above: To make uploads easier, you can add a Google Drive folder to your physical machines.

Installing Drive on Your Machine

To add Drive to your machine, you'll need to re-enter your username and password and set up some basic preferences that include whether you want to sync everything offline, or only certain files.

Accessing Offline

Once downloaded, you'll be able to save files directly into your offline Google Drive. A Drive icon will also be added to your machine's top menu, letting you access your files whenever you like.

KEEPING FILES UP TO DATE

Don't worry that your files won't be up to date the next time you log on to your machine. Whenever you access the internet, your Google Drive will automatically sync and update documents that had been edited offline.

GOING OFFLINE ON MOBILE

You can store files offline on mobile too. To do this, you'll need to download individual files by toggling the 'Available offline' switch to 'on' in the file's own options menu. All offline files are then stored in a dedicated folder on your device.

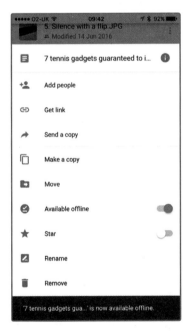

Above: Documents and folders can be downloaded for offline access when you know internet access is going to be scarce.

Above: All offline files can be viewed in their own offline folder.

The ease & simplic
of Gmail, available
across devices

CREATE AN ACCOUNT

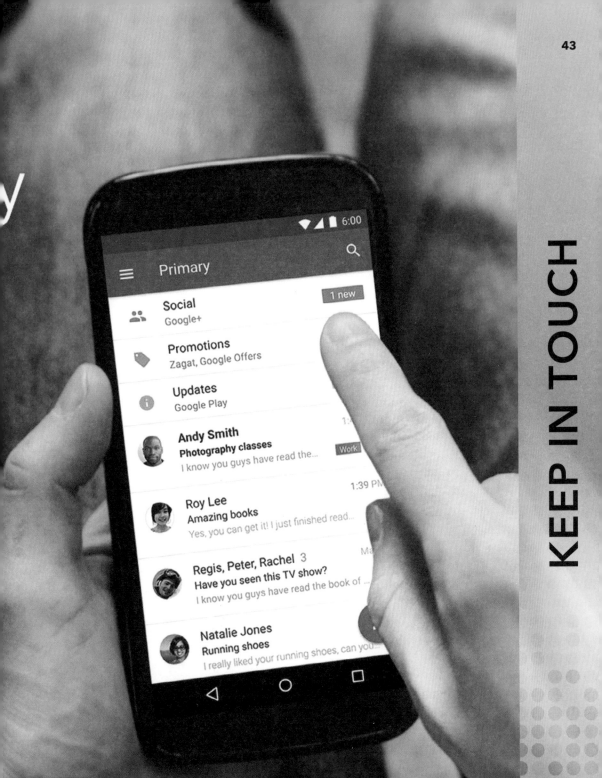

KEEP IN TOUCH

GET CONNECTED WITH GOOGLE APPS

Communicating with friends, family and colleagues has never been easier. This chapter is all about using Gmail and Calendar to make your life as simple and organized as possible. Here we'll show you how to send and receive emails, add attachments and schedule meetings and events.

ALL ABOUT GMAIL

Gmail is the world's most popular email service, with more than 1 billion active monthly users, because it's free and easy to use. Once you've created your Google account, your username (for example, lukejohnsontest) will become the prefix for your Gmail email address (so lukejohnsontest@gmail.com). To access your Gmail inbox you'll need to log in.

Take action right from the inbox

Track packages, review products, RSVP for events and more without opening any emails.

Above: Gmail is Google's email service and lets you keep in touch with friends, family and colleagues.

Selecting the 'Stay signed in' box before entering your password will save you having to sign in on that machine every time.

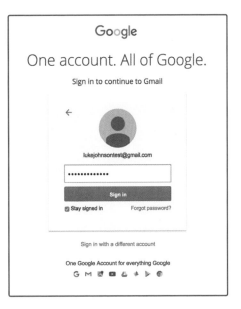

Above: To sign into Gmail, you'll need your account name.

ACCESSING YOUR INBOX

To access your Gmail inbox, first you'll need to visit www.gmail.com and follow these simple steps:

1. Type your email address or username into the box provided at gmail.com and click 'Next'. If you haven't got one already, you'll need to follow the steps on pages 19–20.

2. Enter your password in the box and click on 'Sign in'.

3. If you want to remain signed in and avoid going through this process every time, you can tick the 'Stay signed in' box beneath your password.

Above: You'll also have to type in your secure password.

GETTING TO KNOW GMAIL

When you sign into Gmail, you'll be sent directly to your inbox. This is where you can see all the messages you've been sent.

UNDERSTANDING YOUR INBOX

There are a lot of different buttons and menus in the Gmail inbox. Here is what they all mean:

1 **Search:** The search bar lets you search your email for specific messages, contacts or keywords.

2 **Compose:** Clicking this button will open a new blank email you can use to send messages.

3 **Starred:** Important emails can be 'starred' to mark them as important. This is where all starred emails are stored.

4 **Sent mail:** Here you can see a list of all the emails you've sent.

5 **Drafts:** Emails you've started but not sent can be found under this tab.

6 **More:** Clicking this drop-down menu brings up new inbox folders, including emails that have been marked as spam and those you've previously deleted.

7 **Recent chats:** Here you can see recent instant messaging chat conversations you've had with friends using Google Hangouts.

8 **Primary:** This is your main inbox, where you'll be able to find all of your latest, most important emails.

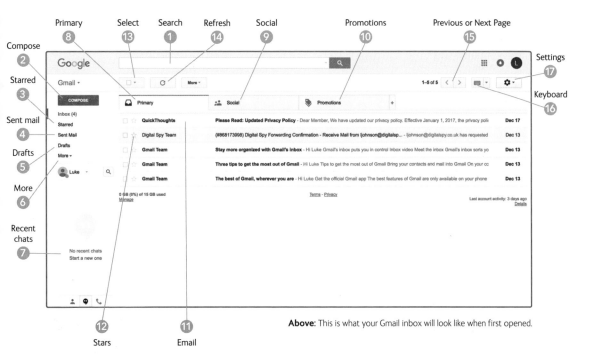

Compose **2**

Starred **3**

Sent mail **4**

Drafts **5**

More **6**

Recent chats **7**

Primary **8**

Select **13**

Search **1**

Refresh **14**

Social **9**

Promotions **10**

Previous or Next Page **15**

Settings **17**

Keyboard **16**

Stars **12**

Email **11**

Above: This is what your Gmail inbox will look like when first opened.

9 **Social:** If your email address is connected to social media accounts such as Facebook and Twitter, their email alerts will live here to keep your inbox free for more important messages.

10 **Promotions:** Unsolicited sales and promotional emails from retailers will land here to stop your primary inbox becoming cluttered.

11 **Email:** This is an individual email. It shows you who sent it, the subject and the time it was received.

12 **Stars:** Clicking these small stars marks individual emails as important and adds them to your 'Starred' folder.

13 **Select**: Clicking this box lets you select up to 50 emails at a time. Once selected, you can delete or move them more easily.

14 **Refresh**: Expecting a new email? Clicking this refreshes the inbox.

15 **Previous or Next Page**: When you have lots of emails, clicking these arrows will take you forwards and backwards a page at a time.

16 **Keyboard**: Pressing this icon lets you change the language of your inbox.

17 **Settings**: This menu offers advanced options for customizing your inbox. In here you can change the layout, background colours and how your emails are displayed.

WORKING WITH MESSAGES

Now you know your way around the inbox, it's time to start sending and receiving emails. Here we will show you the basics of creating, deleting and managing email.

COMPOSING AN EMAIL

Above: Composing a new email can be achieved within the Gmail inbox.

1. Hit that big, red 'Compose' button in the top-left corner of your Gmail inbox.

2. When the pop-up template window appears, enter the email address of your desired recipient in the 'To' box. If they are already stored in your contacts list, start typing their name and Gmail will find them.

3. Add an email subject. This helps recipients know what's inside before opening the email.

4. The main box is where you type out your message.

5. Press that bright blue 'Send' button at the bottom of the window. That's it. You just sent your first email!

RECEIVING EMAIL

Now you've learnt to send emails, all you've got to do is wait for the replies to come rolling in. Pleasingly, receiving emails is even easier than sending them. You literally have to do nothing.

Checking Your Received Email

You'll know you've got a new email, as it will show with a white rather than grey background in your inbox.

Opening Emails

To open a new message, you simply need to click on it, and can do this by clicking on any part of the notifying bar. Whether you click the sender's name, email subject or date/time received, all have the same effect of opening the email.

What Your Email Will Look Like

Once open, you'll see your received email in full. The main body will sit beneath the sender's details and the exact time it was received. If any attachments, such as pictures or documents, have been added, these will be shown at the bottom, beneath any written message.

Above: When you first open Gmail, you'll have an email from Google explaining the features.

Above: You can reply to an email by clicking the reply arrow at the top or 'click here to reply' at the bottom.

REPLYING TO EMAILS

Once you've read your email, it's time to reply. This doesn't have to mean creating a completely new email though. Instead, you can click a single button and have your response follow directly on from the original communication. This starts what is called an email chain, with all past communications following on in a single thread.

How to Reply

1. Open your desired email.

2. Locate the left-pointing curved arrow next to the email's received date in the upper-right corner.

3. Press this button and write your reply in the new email box that appears.

FORWARDING RECEIVED EMAILS

Sometimes you'll want to send someone an email that you've been sent yourself; this is called forwarding. Fortunately, you don't have to type out the whole message again. Instead there is a dedicated forwarding button that will do it all for you with just one click.

How to Forward an Email

To forward an email, you'll need to do the following:

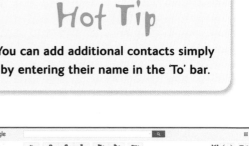

Above: To forward a message on to a contact, you'll need to click the down button next to the return arrow.

1. Open the email you want to forward.

2. Click the down arrow next to the reply button; this will launch a drop-down menu of options.

3. Select 'Forward', the second option down.

4. Enter the name or names of the contacts you want to forward the email to.

5. You have the option to add to the email with your own comments. This is entered in the main body box.

6. Click on the blue 'Send' button at the bottom of the email.

Hot Tip

Keep an eye on file sizes. Gmail will only let you add attachments up to 25mb in size per message.

Above: You can attach files to emails by clicking the paperclip icon.

Above: To send an email, just click the 'Send' button.

EMAIL ATTACHMENTS

Emails don't have to be boring, text-heavy affairs. They can be used to send and receive all manner of attachments too. From pictures to documents, videos to presentations, your emails can be used to transport and share pretty much everything you need. Assuming you know how.

Uploading Attachments

If you want to send files in emails, you need to attach them. You can do this by clicking the small paperclip icon at the bottom of the email you're composing. This will let you select files from your machine. Once you've found the right one, selecting it will start the upload process.

Downloading Attachments

Received attachments are shown at the bottom of emails. Hovering over the file icons will give you the option to either download them to your machine or save directly to your Google Drive, for viewing whenever needed. If you click on the attachment, it will open a preview version for you to see, again with the options to download or save to Google Drive, as well as to open in different applications, print and more. Click outside the preview to return to the email.

MANAGING YOUR MESSAGES

You've got the basics, now it's time to start managing your growing number of emails. Here we'll talk you through creating folders, moving and deleting your unwanted mail and how to access your email on multiple devices.

CREATING NEW FOLDERS

If you really want to manage your messages, you're going to need to create some custom folders. Having Starred and Social folders is fine, but how about folders especially for your bills, pictures of the family or one that looks after all your shopping? Sounds useful, right?

Making a Folder

To make a folder, just follow these simple steps:

Above: Managing your emails is made easier by creating new folders known as 'labels'

1. Click 'More' on the left-hand run of inbox options.

2. Select the 'Create new label' option.

3. Give your folder a useful name like 'Bills' or 'Shopping' and click 'Create'.

4. You should now see your new folder alongside the 'Inbox' and 'Drafts' tabs.

MOVING MESSAGES

With folders made, it's easier to move and file messages. There are number of ways to do this but the easiest is directly from the inbox. Click the 'select' square next to the desired message and at the top of the inbox a folder-shaped icon will appear. Clicking this will let you choose which folder you want the message sent to.

Hot Tip

See that list of email folders on the left-hand side? You can simply drag messages from your inbox list into any of these.

Don't want to keep your message? Fine, delete it and reduce the clutter in your inbox. You can do this while in the message just by clicking the trashcan icon above the body of the email itself. You can also delete messages in bulk by selecting them from the main inbox and clicking the same trashcan icon.

Above: To delete a message, you'll need to click the trashcan icon.

USING GMAIL ON THE MOVE

Thanks to smartphones and tablets, Gmail doesn't have to keep you locked to your desk. You can now take your email with you.

GMAIL APPS

As well as being able to register your Gmail account on your phone's native email app, a dedicated Gmail app is available for iOS and Android. This offers enhanced features that more closely resemble those on the desktop. It's free to download.

CUSTOMIZING GMAIL

If you find Gmail is all looking a bit sanitized and serious for your liking, you can change it. Under the Settings tab is an array of customization options. You can have fewer or more emails per page, and add a colourful or picture-led background theme to liven up your inbox.

Right: You can customize your Gmail experience by selecting a custom theme.

GETTING TO GRIPS WITH CALENDARS

Just because you've discovered emails doesn't mean you have to stop talking to people face to face. Fortunately, Google's Calendar app will let you manage all of your social and professional meetings in one place. Here we'll introduce you to the skills you'll need to use Calendar efficiently.

UNDERSTANDING THE LAYOUT

To get the most out of the Calendar app, you need to know what all the tabs mean. Here's a handy guide.

1. **Create**: Clicking this allows you to create a new calendar entry or event.

2. **Month view**: Here you can scroll through months at a time. Clicking a specific date will take you to a view of that day's activities.

3. **My calendars**: You can create multiple calendars, such as personal and work ones, and switch between them or view them all together here.

4. **Other calendars**: You can also view friends' calendars that have been shared with you here, as well as browse Interesting Calendars to add other dates, like regional holidays, sporting events and esoteric items such as phases of the moon.

5. **Today**: Clicking this will jump your calendar to the current date.

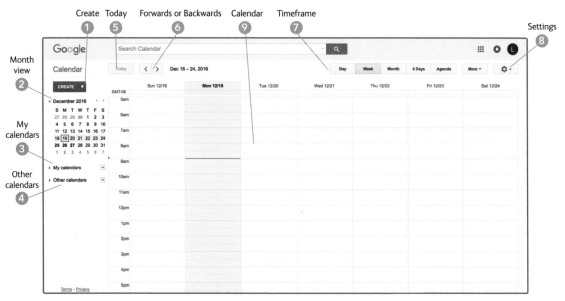

Above: Your Google Calendar lets you input meetings and reminders any time of any day.

6 **Forwards or Backwards**: Clicking these will take you forwards or backwards through days, weeks or months.

7 **Timeframe**: These buttons let you pick how long a period you want your main calendar to display at any one time.

8 **Settings**: In here you can change elements of your calendar and access more advanced features.

9 **Calendar**: The calendar itself takes pride of place and is broken down hour by hour.

Hot Tip

Add the Gmail and Calendar apps to your phone and Gmail will automatically pull emailed reservations for things such as flights, concerts or restaurants into your calendar.

ADDING EVENTS

To add a new event, you need to click that big, red 'Create' button in the top-left corner of your calendar. When adding a new event, you're able to customize it with all manner of details:

- The name of the event, such as 'Dinner with Alice'.

- The date it's taking place.

- Its start and end time.

- The location of the event.

- A description of what will be happening.

Hot Tip

Plans just moved to the following day? Just drag your event across the calendar instead of fiddling with a new time and date.

Above: Quick Adds let you make speedy calendar additions with only minimal details.

QUICK ADDS

No time to mess around with the particulars? Don't worry, you can quickly add calendar reminders simply by telling Google what's going on. Click the down arrow next to the 'Create' button and you can type in an event, such as 'Football with Mike next Saturday at 3pm'. Amazingly, Google's smart enough to understand this context and add a suitable calendar reminder. Seriously, try it.

EDITING EVENTS

Plans change. You know it, we know it and fortunately so does Google. Because of this, you can edit all elements of your scheduled events whenever you like. How? Just click on the entry in your calendar. This will open the creation page, letting you tweak times, location and, well, anything else you want.

CREATING CALENDARS

If you want to create a new calendar, you can and it will appear alongside your main calendar, just in a new colour. Follow these simple steps:

1. Find 'My calendars' on the left of the calendar view and click the small down arrow next to it.

2. Click 'Create new calendar'.

3. Input a calendar name such as 'office schedule' and, if wanted, a brief description.

Above: You can create multiple calendars that overlap on the same time board in different colours.

4. Once you press 'Create Calendar' your new calendar should appear under your 'My calendars' tab and you can start adding events and appointments.

SHARING CALENDARS

As well as creating new calendars, you can share existing ones. This lets a whole family, friendship group or work team manage their time together and let everyone involved see what the others are up to, and when.

Above: Sharing calendars is great to make sure everyone is on the same schedule.

How Do You Share a Calendar?

To share a calendar, you need to follow these steps:

1. Click 'My calendars' on the left of your main calendar.

2. Select the calendar you wish to share from the drop-down list and click the down arrow next to it.

3. Click the 'Share this calendar' option.

4. Enter the names/emails of all the people with whom you wish to share the calendar.

5. When you click 'Save', an invitation to edit will be sent to your desired recipients.

Above: The Google Calendar is also available as a smartphone app.

CHECKING YOUR CALENDAR ON THE GO

Like Gmail, the Google Calendar app doesn't have to be locked to your desktop. You can access all your appointments on the go using the free-to-download smartphone app.

Finding the App

Called simply Google Calendar, the app is available in both the iOS App Store and Android's Google Play Store. Once downloaded, if you've already synced your Google account to your phone, your calendars will instantly be transported across.

Never Miss an Appointment

As your calendar is stored in the cloud, there's no limit to the devices you can access it on. As well as your laptop and phone, you can see your calendar events on your tablet, smartwatch and even TV.

Hot Tip

If you've set a location for an event, the mobile app will use a map of the location as a backdrop for the event window.

GETTING TO KNOW GOOGLE HANGOUTS

Google doesn't just let you send emails. It's time to explore its instant messaging service, Hangouts. Here we'll explain how to connect with your contacts quickly and look at sending and receiving Hangouts messages on your computer, phone or tablet.

WHAT IS HANGOUTS?

Similar to Facebook Messenger or WhatsApp, Hangouts is an instant messaging service that lets you send messages, images and files to contacts instantly, without the formality of creating a full email. Instant messages are similar to text messages and can be sent and received on a number of devices, and Hangouts can include one person or many.

Above: Hangouts is Google's own instant messaging service, much like WhatsApp or Facebook Messenger.

HOW DO YOU USE IT?

You can make use of Hangouts in a number of ways. There's a Hangouts panel in your Gmail inbox and a dedicated website (hangouts.google.com). You can also download the free Hangouts app to your smartphone and tablet for messages on the move.

INSTALLING THE APP

Hangouts is available as a free-to-download app for both iOS and Android operating systems. This means you can use it on any smartphone or tablet whenever you've got a Wi-Fi or cellular signal. To add the app to your phone or tablet, you'll need to do the following:

1. Locate the Google Hangouts app within the App Store or Google Play Store.

2. Select download and enter your iTunes or Google password.

3. Once downloaded, follow the sign-in process using your Google log-in details.

USING HANGOUTS

As Hangouts is so quick and is available on so many different devices, it's a great tool for improving business communications or simply staying in touch with friends.

Starting a Hangout with Gmail

Hangouts can be held between you and one other person or multiple people. Starting one, however, works the same no matter how many are involved. Want to start a Hangouts conversation from within Gmail? This is how you do it:

1. Log in to Gmail and locate the Hangouts panel on the left of the inbox.

2. Click 'Start a new one' in the chat panel.

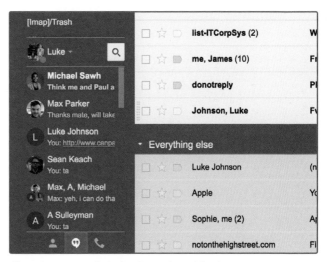

Above: Hangouts can also be found as a side panel directly within Gmail.

3. In the pop-up window, enter the name of the contact or contacts you want to chat with.

4. Enter your conversation greeting and select 'Send invite' to open the conversation.

Hangouts on the App
Prefer to use the app to chat? This is what you need to do:

1. Open the app and enter your Google account details to log in.

2. Click on the large '+' icon to open a conversation window.

3. Enter the name of your desired contact to communicate with an individual, or press 'New group' to add multiple contacts.

4. Write your message and press send.

COMMUNICATING IN HANGOUTS
As well as being able to send text-message style communications, Hangouts lets you send a whole host of other information and attachments.

What Can You Send in Hangouts?
The list of things you can send in Hangouts is long, but includes the following:

○ Photographs

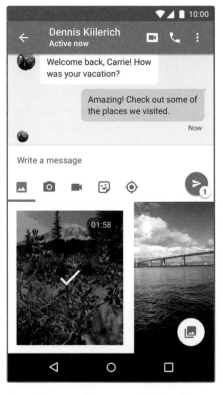

Above: You can install Hangouts on your phone for on-the-move messaging.

- Documents

- Emoji and stickers

- Videos

- Your current location on Google Maps

> **Hot Tip**
>
> **When your contact's little round profile image moves below your message it means they've seen and read it.**

HANGOUT'S OTHER USES

Offering many services in one, Hangouts can replace a number of the apps on your phone with its additional features. Icons at the bottom of chat windows let you make voice and even video calls, all within Hangouts.

Above: As well as typing messages, Hangouts lets you host free video calls, much like Skype or FaceTime.

WORK TOGETHER

GETTING STARTED WITH GOOGLE DOCS AND SHEETS

Docs and Sheets are the two most popular Google apps. Google's answer to Microsoft Word and Excel, they let you create text documents and spreadsheets respectively, and share your creations with friends and colleagues.

It's easy to start working with Google Docs, and once you're going, you'll never look back. Here we'll show you how to make the most of the features Docs has to offer.

WHAT IS GOOGLE DOCS?

Docs is Google's answer to Microsoft Word. It is free word-processing software that lets you create text documents that can be enhanced by the inclusion of tables, charts and pictures. It's the essential tool for business proposals and quick to-do lists alike, and a program you'll quickly find it hard to live without.

ACCESSING GOOGLE DOCS

Google Docs is easy to find. You can access it either via your Google Drive, or by directing your browser directly to docs.google.com. This will take you to your Google Docs homepage, an area where you can see all your existing Docs files and create new ones at the click of a button.

Hot Tip

Planning on creating a brochure, writing your CV or drafting a formal letter? Instead of opening a blank document, have a look at Google's Docs templates for easy editing of preset designs.

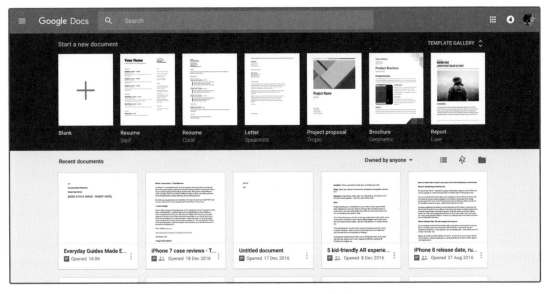

Above: Google's answer to Microsoft Word, Google Docs lets you store documents in the cloud.

CREATING A NEW DOCUMENT

Creating a new document in Google Docs couldn't be easier. Once you've pointed your browser at docs.google.com, clicking the big 'blank' button under the 'Start a new document' heading at the top of the page will create a new blank document.

Right: You can create a new document by clicking the large 'Blank' tab in the top-left corner.

OPENING EXISTING DOCUMENTS

All of your previously created Google Docs files sit in date order on your Docs homepage. Simply clicking on any one of these will reopen it, letting you make all of the alterations and additions you want.

Editing a Document

There are dozens of ways you can edit your document, but the most common is to simply start typing. When you open a new document, the cursor will automatically fall on the body of the document. When you start to type, your edits will automatically appear.

Where's the Save Button?

Don't worry, you're not going mad not being able to find it – as Google Docs are stored online, there is no traditional save button. Don't worry though, the software will automatically save your documents after each and every update you make. Like magic, by the time you stop typing, your changes will have been saved.

Above: A number of design templates can help you save time creating certain types of files.

FORMATTING GOOGLE DOCS

Once you've opened a new document, it's time to start learning what all of those buttons do. Here's a quick guide.

1 **Undo**: Clicking this will undo the last edit you made.

2 **Redo**: Changed your mind? Click this button to change it back again.

3 **Paint format**: This lets you copy the formatting of certain text – such as type of font, font size and colour – and paint it on to other sections of text.

Above: A blank Google Docs document looks very much like a standard Word document.

④ **Zoom:** Here you can zoom in or out of the page.

⑤ **Styles:** Here you can choose the format of the text, changing its size and style to a number of presets.

⑥ **Font:** Clicking here lets you select the font you want to use.

⑦ **Font size:** And here you can choose the size of your font.

⑧ **Bold:** Clicking here will make the selected text bold.

⑨ **Italic:** Selecting this will italicize your selected text.

⑩ **Underline:** Click here to underline your selected text.

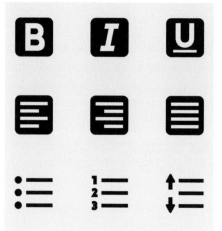

⑪ **Text colour:** You can change the colour of selected text by clicking here.

⑫ **Alignment:** These four options let you choose if your text is aligned to the left, centre, right or fully justified across the page.

⑬ **Line spacing:** You can increase or decrease the space between lines of text using this key.

⑭ **Numbered list:** Clicking here will insert a numbered list.

⑮ **Bulleted list:** Selecting this will add bullet points to your document.

⑯ **Clear formatting:** You can return everything to basic text by clicking this button.

INSERTING ITEMS

It's not just text that you can add to your documents. Google Docs lets you add all manner of images, tables and charts too. Here's how.

ADDING AN IMAGE

Adding images to your documents can help illustrate the points you're trying to make. Docs lets you add images wherever you like in just a couple of clicks:

1. Click 'Insert' on the top menu run.

2. Select 'Image' from the drop-down list.

3. Choose an image stored on your machine to upload, take a new photo, or drag your desired image across from a web page.

Above: Docs aren't just for words, you can add images too.

4. Your image should now appear within your document. You can resize it by dragging the image markings at its corner in or out.

ADDING A TABLE

Adding a table follows a similar process to images, albeit with a bit of additional customization. To insert one, you'll need to follow these steps:

1. Click 'Insert' on the top menu run.

2. Scroll down and hover over the 'Table' option.

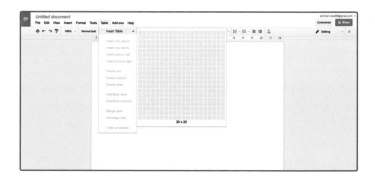

3. Drag your mouse over the grid that appears on the right;

Above: Custom tables can be created with however many rows and columns you need.

the wider you drag, the more rows and columns you'll see added.

4. Once you've chosen the number of rows and columns to display, click on the square in the bottom-right corner of your grid template.

5. Your table should now appear within your document.

ADDING A LINK

Sometimes, your document needs to feature internet links to add context or offer additional reading. These are called hyperlinks. They can be added by doing the following:

1. Highlight the word or section of text you'd like to attach the link to.

2. Click the 'Insert link' button on the top menu run (it looks like three small chain links).

3. Paste your desired link in the pop-up window and click 'Apply'.

4. Now when you or others click this highlighted section of text, the target web page will automatically open up.

GOOGLE DOCS KEYBOARD SHORTCUTS

There are a number of keyboard shortcuts that can help speed up the editing process:

Keyboard Command	Shortcut
Ctrl + C	Copy selected text
Ctrl + A	Select all text
Ctrl + X	Cut selected text
Ctrl + V	Paste selected item
Ctrl + B	Bold selected text
Ctrl + I	Italicize selected text
Ctrl + U	Underline selected text
Ctrl + O	Open existing file
Ctrl + P	Print selected document
Ctrl + Z	Undo last edit
Ctrl + Y	Redo last edit
Ctrl + Shift + H	Find and replace specific words with alternative
Ctrl + K	Add link to selected text
Ctrl + Enter	Add page break
Ctrl + \	Remove formatting from selected text
Ctrl + Shift + Y	Define selected word
Ctrl + Shift + C	Show word count
Ctrl + (+) or Ctrl + (-)	Zoom in or out of text

More Keyboard Shortcuts

Further keyboard shortcuts can be found by pressing Ctrl + / at the same time.

Right: Keyboard shortcuts can help you complete regular tasks more quickly.

Keyboard shortcuts	Search all shortcuts		View all shortcuts in Help Centre	×
Popular keyboard shortcuts				
Text formatting				
Bold		⌘B		
Italic		⌘I		
Underline		⌘U		
Strike-through		Option+Shift+5		
Superscript		⌘.		
Subscript		⌘,		

MASTERING THE TOOLS

There are multiple tools hidden within Google Docs that can help make your life easier. It's time to start getting to grips with them.

PRINT YOUR DOCUMENTS

To print your document, do one of the following:

○ Click the printer icon on the top menu run.

○ Click 'File' on the top menu, and select 'Print' from the drop-down menu.

○ Press 'Ctrl + P' on your keyboard.

Above: When printing a document, you'll be given a preview of what it will look like.

KEEP TRACK OF YOUR WORDS

If you're writing to a word limit, you can check your document's word count by clicking on the 'Tools' menu and selecting 'Word count' from the drop-down bar.

Hot Tip

Use Mac not PC? All the same keyboard shortcuts can be used by replacing 'Ctrl' with

CHECK YOUR SPELLING

Spell check has been the saviour of many a business plan. To find misspelled words in your document, select 'Spelling' from the 'Tools' menu. This will open a pop-up window that will take you through your spelling mistakes one by one.

SHARE YOUR DOCUMENT

You can share your document with others simply by selecting the 'Share' option from the 'File' menu. Once selected, you'll have to state whom you want to share the document with before a link is sent to your desired recipients.

Above: Like your folders, you can share individual documents with other people.

Collaborate with Others

If you want to be able to collaborate with others, you can give them permission to edit the document when you share it. If multiple people are working in the same document simultaneously, you'll be able to watch their updates in real time. Each user will be given their own colour-coded cursor.

USE DOCS ON MULTIPLE DEVICES

Like Gmail, using Google Docs doesn't restrict you to using a single, stationary machine. With all of your files stored in the cloud, you can access them on any internet-connected machine, anywhere in the world. This doesn't just mean desktop computers and laptops either. Dedicated Google Docs smartphone and tablet apps mean you can also create, edit and share documents while on the go.

Google Docs on the Move

Available as free downloads, searching for 'Google Docs' in either the iOS App Store or Google Play Store will let you fill your phone or tablet with Google's word-processing software.

Integrating Docs with Other Google Apps

Google lets you download add-ons to plug into Docs. These are pieces of software developed by both Google and third parties that add enhanced features, such as a thesaurus, Google Translate and a keyboard for adding accents to letters. They can be found under the 'Add-ons' menu.

Above: Smartphone apps let you access your Google Docs files on Android or iOS.

WORKING WITH GOOGLE SHEETS

If you need to create a spreadsheet, Sheets is the Google app you'll need to use. Like Microsoft Excel, it offers a pre-made spreadsheet that you can customize with your own columns, fields and charts. They can be used to track everything from sales figures to shopping or to-do lists.

ACCESSING GOOGLE SHEETS

Like Docs, Google Sheets can be accessed either through a dedicated tab on your Google Drive homepage, or by pointing your browser at the dedicated holding page – sheets.google.com.

Hot Tip

Pre-made templates make it easier if you're looking to create a work schedule, budget sheet or calendar.

CREATING A NEW SPREADSHEET

Once again, creating a new spreadsheet is pleasingly easy thanks to Google Sheets. Once on the Sheets homepage, click the large 'Blank' button under the 'Start a new spreadsheet' header in the top-left corner of the page.

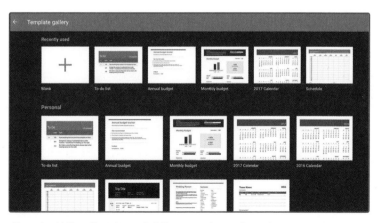

Above: As with Docs, Sheets lets you build forms around pre-made templates.

ENTERING DATA

Each square on your new spreadsheet is called a cell. To enter data, you must first select the cell you are looking to edit. You can do this just by clicking on it, then you can enter data either by typing directly into the cell, pasting previously copied content or inserting a function or formula – two areas we will cover a little later.

Autocompleting

If you're regularly entering the same data into cells, such as the name of a supplier or member of staff, you can enable autocomplete to speed the process up. Activated under the 'Tools' menu, it will look at your most regularly used cells and suggest these when it notices you're typing them again.

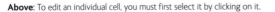

Above: To edit an individual cell, you must first select it by clicking on it.

EDITING CELLS

If you decide you want to change what's in one of your cells, you can edit it. Just clicking on a cell and starting to type will completely replace the content already there.

Being More Precise

To manually change parts of what's already in a cell, you must first double-click it. This will place the cursor directly within the cell and let you move around and edit the existing text without deleting the cell's content.

FORMATTING YOUR SPREADSHEET

There are a number of ways to format your spreadsheet. Some you'll recognize from Google Docs, others, like the following, are exclusive to the needs of Sheets.

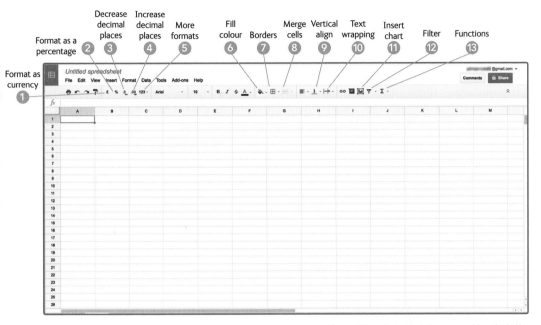

Above: This is what a blank Sheets spreadsheet looks like.

1 **Format as currency**: Clicking this will transform numbers in the selected cells into monetary figures with the currency symbol you request.

2 **Format as a percentage**: This turns numbers into a percentage.

3 **Decrease decimal places**: Every time you click this, one decimal place will be removed from your figure.

4 **Increase decimal places**: Each click on this button adds a decimal place to your figure.

5 **More formats**: This button opens a drop-down menu of additional format options, including date, time and plain text.

6 **Fill colour**: This lets you fill selected cells with the colour of your choice.

7 **Borders**: You can change the thickness and visibility of borders on selected cells here.

8 **Merge cells**: After highlighting a number of cells, clicking this button will merge them into a single, large cell.

9 **Vertical align**: This button lets you choose where in the cell your text sits.

10 **Text wrapping**: Clicking this helps large sections of text fit in a box by putting it on multiple lines.

11 **Insert chart**: You can add charts and graphs by clicking this button.

12 **Filter**: This button lets you organize cells in a number of ways of your choosing. You can show content in ascending or descending order by alphabetical or numerical values.

13 **Functions**: Clicking this lets you add equations to cells. You can create the sum of a certain range of cells or find the average value without having to figure it out yourself.

UNDERSTANDING COLUMNS AND ROWS

There are a number of ways to edit the columns and rows of your spreadsheet that have nothing to do with simply inputting data:

Change Their Size

You can alter the size of columns and rows just by dragging their borders. If you hover over the edge you wish to make bigger, an arrow will appear. Clicking and dragging will let you resize the entire column or row.

Resize to Fit

If you want to resize a column or row to fit content that's already been added, double-clicking this highlighted edge will snap the entire run of cells to the size of the one that's most full.

Delete the Lot

If you want to delete an entire column or row, you can do so in a couple of clicks. This won't

Above: You can manipulate multiple columns at once – and all their accompanying cells – by dragging to select them.

just empty the cells, but completely remove them from your sheet. If you right-click the section you want to remove, a pop-up menu will give you a number of options, including delete. So to delete column C, you'd right-click the 'C' at the top and select 'Delete column'.

Add More

There are nearly endless rows and columns on your blank spreadsheet. If you want to add one in a specific place, however, such as between two existing rows, you can. To do this, right-click the column or row where you want to insert a new one and select the options. New rows can be inserted above or below existing ones, with columns slotting in either to the left or right.

Hot Tip

Changed your mind on a delete? Press Ctrl + Z on your keyboard to instantly undo the last change.

Above: You can copy, move or delete entire rows by right-clicking on them.

FORMULAS, FUNCTIONS AND CHARTS

Once you've got the hang of the spreadsheet basics, you can build on your creation with all manner of formulas, functions and charts. Here's what you need to know.

UNDERSTANDING FUNCTIONS

Functions are a selection of pre-made formulas that let you do things like add up figures in a number of cells instantly. They don't require any special coding; all the work has been done for you.

Making Use of Them

You can add functions simply by clicking the 'Functions' button on the top menu bar. Once you've picked the function you want, you can highlight the cells you want the calculation to include. Once cells have been selected, the result should instantly appear.

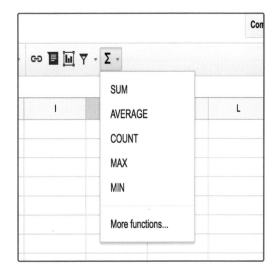

Above: Formulas complete complex calculations without any faff.

CREATING CHARTS

Your spreadsheets don't need to be boring lines of text and data – you can visualize your information with a range of charts and graphs. These can be used to show everything from sales performances to changing spends over certain timeframes.

Inserting Charts

To insert a chart, highlight the data and cells you want to visualize and click the 'Insert chart' button on the top menu. You'll then be able to select the type of chart you want to use, such as bar graph, pie chart or line graph. Google Sheets will recommend certain types of chart, depending on the data selected.

Editing Your Chart

Once created, you can edit all elements of your chart, from choosing its colour schemes to adding labels and annotations. You can move your charts across your sheet just by clicking and dragging it.

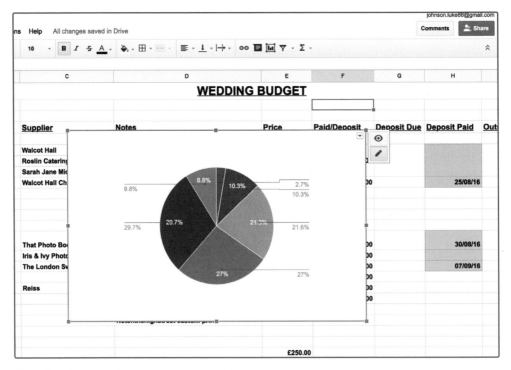

Above: Sheets lets you transform your data into a variety of charts.

REFINING AND SHARING

There's still more you can change about your spreadsheet, including what it looks like and who can view it.

VIEWING AND CORRECTING

Removing Gridline View
All those grid lines can be helpful. They can be pretty distracting and confusing too. You can remove them for a cleaner, less cluttered sheet. To do this, you'll need to click the 'View' menu and select 'Gridlines'.

Check Your Spelling
Like in Docs, you can use spell check to keep an eye on typos. To activate, click 'Spelling' under the 'Tools' menu.

Above: You can also remove all gridlines for a cleaner, less cluttered view.

Above: As with other Google Apps, Sheets lets you share your creations with others.

SHARING YOUR SHEETS

If you want other people to have access to the spreadsheet you've created, you can share it with them. To do this, you will need to select the 'Share' button found under the 'File' menu. Here you can enter the details of whom you want to share the spreadsheet with.

Collaborating with Others

Sharing your sheets doesn't have to just be about letting people see what you've done. You can give them permission to collaborate on the same document with you. To do this you'll need to select the 'Can edit' option from the list. Now you'll be able to work on the sheet at the same time as others, seeing at all times what your collaborators are doing.

PRINTING YOUR SHEET

Sharing your sheet doesn't have to be digital – you can print physical copies too. To do this, you need to select 'Print' from the 'File' menu. Once in the print menu, you have a few decisions to make, including paper orientation, whether you want your sheet compressed to a page or split across many, and whether or not gridlines should be printed.

USING SHEETS OFFLINE

Like Docs, you can download your sheets so you can access and edit them offline. To do this, you'll need to have installed Drive on your machine. You can also download your sheet as an Excel-compatible file if you want to transfer it to another machine. You can do this under the 'Download as' tab in the 'File' menu.

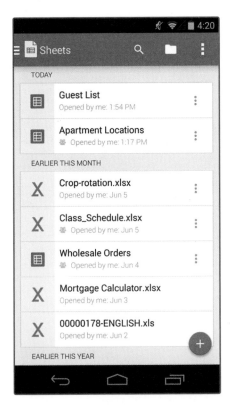

USE SHEETS ON MULTIPLE DEVICES

You can use Sheets on a number of machines. Dedicated Google Sheets smartphone and tablet apps are available, for free, on both iOS and Android. What's more, as your sheets are stored in the cloud, you can access them on multiple connected machines simultaneously.

Integrating Sheets with Other Google Apps

You can integrate a number of additional apps with Sheets. To find and add these, you can click 'Add-ons' on the top menu bar.

Left: Sheets is also available on your smartphone thanks to a free app.

CREATE AND PRESENT

GETTING CREATIVE

As well as giving you the tools to be practical and productive, Google apps can also help to get your creative juices flowing. Here we'll look at how the Slides, Sites and Forms apps can be used to create everything from presentations to your very first website.

GETTING TO KNOW SLIDES

Slides is Google's answer to Microsoft PowerPoint. It gives you the ability to create presentations and slide shows that can then be shared with or displayed to others. These can be useful for work presentations or creating fun slides to show your holiday photos.

CREATING A PRESENTATION

You can create a blank presentation directly from your Google Drive homepage just by selecting 'Slides' from under the 'New' options. You can also create presentations directly from your main Slides page at slides.google.com.

If you've opted to start with a completely blank presentation, you'll

Left: Slides is Google's answer to Microsoft PowerPoint and lets you create presentations.

need to build it up layer by layer, including picking its theme, layout and what content it displays.

Deciding on a Theme

When you open a blank presentation, the right-hand panel will show a selection of themes. These change the base design of each and every slide in your presentation. Available themes range from simply black and white slides to more stylized options.

Picking a Theme

To select a theme, just click on it. This will see it instantly appear on your presentation.

Hot Tip

Make use of Google's pre-built Slides templates for fast, easy, good-looking presentations.

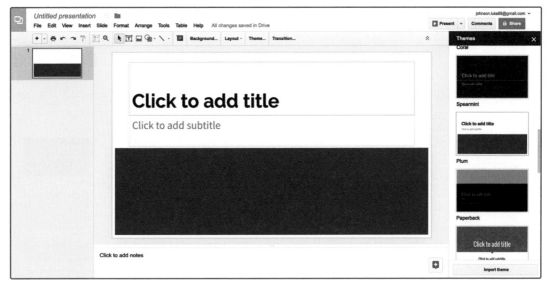

Above: When creating a presentation, you can select a theme.

UNDERSTANDING YOUR PRESENTATION

As it's used to create very different things from Docs and Sheets, Slides plays host to a number of its own shortcut and menu buttons. Here is what they all do.

1 New slide: Every time you click this button, an additional slide will be added to your presentation.

2 Print: Clicking here will print a copy of your presentation.

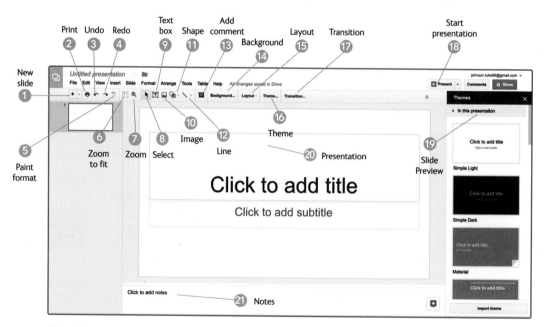

Above: This is what a blank Slide looks like.

(3) Undo: You can undo your last edit by pressing this button.

(4) Redo: If you change your mind, you can redo the edit with this button.

(5) Paint format: You can copy and paste the formatting behind elements using this feature.

(6) Zoom to fit: Pressing this will make an entire slide visible on screen.

(7) Zoom: You can zoom in and out using this button.

(8) Select: You'll need this button to select individual elements of busy slides.

(9) Text box: This button lets you add text boxes to your presentation.

(10) Image: You can start inserting images into your presentation using this button.

(11) Shape: Press this and you can draw shapes on to your presentation.

(12) Line: You can draw lines on to your presentation using this button.

(13) Add comment: This button lets you add comments for contributors to see.

(14) Background: Pressing this lets you alter elements of the slide's background, including design and colour. This can be done for individual slides, or the whole presentation.

(15) Layout: You can change the layout of each slide by clicking this.

Hot Tip

You can hide unwanted menus and give more space to your presentation by clicking the double up arrow to the right of the menu bar.

(16) **Theme:** If you've closed the sidebar, you can alter your presentation theme here.

(17) **Transition:** This button lets you add animated transitions between slides and elements of them.

(18) **Start presentation:** You can preview or start your presentation with this button.

(19) **Slide Preview:** Thumbnail previews of all your slides are shown here.

(20) **Presentation:** This is your presentation; you can see and edit it slide by slide.

(21) **Notes:** You can add presentation notes here. People watching your presentation won't be able to see these.

Above: You can add additional slides to your presentation by clicking the plus symbol.

ADDING SLIDES

To add a new slide, click the plus symbol on the 'New slide' tab of the menu run. There is a variety of types of slide to choose from. You will see your new slide has appeared in the thumbnail list below.

Slide Types

Each theme will offer a variety of slide types. These can be seen and selected by clicking the down arrow next to the 'New slide' button. Available slide types include blank slides, those that act as a title page, section headers, two columns and captioned slides. There are also dedicated templates for big numbers and section title with description.

Duplicating Slides

If you want repeats of the same slide, you can duplicate it. To do this, you'll need to right-click on your desired slide and select the 'Duplicate slide' option from the pop-up menu.

EDITING YOUR PRESENTATION

Once you've added a number of slides, it's time to start editing them and building them up with content, images and animations. Here's how you can do all that.

ADDING CONTENT

Before you can start worrying about animating your slides, first you've got to add a range of content. There's little that you can't add to your presentations, with everything from images and videos to texts, charts and diagrams all possible.

Texting up Your Presentation

You can't just type anywhere on a presentation slide. You need to make sure there's a text box there first. You can add this by clicking the 'Text box' button and physically drawing out the space

Above: You can add text to your presentation by clicking on any of the elements.

in which you want to be able to type. You can resize this later by clicking on the box and dragging its corners in or out.

Adding Images

To add an image, select the 'Image' button from the menu run and choose from your machine the picture you want to insert. Once added, you can drag it to reposition it, or resize it using its corner markings.

ANIMATING YOUR PRESENTATION

Everyone knows the best things about presentations are the cool transitions between slides and the animated elements on them. That's why it's time to learn how to add these.

Slide Transitions

Adding transitions between slides is easy. Simply click a slide and press the 'Transitions' button from the menu run. Now on the left a pop-up window lets you pick the type of transition (fade, slide, flip), whether you want this applied to a single slide or all, and the speed at which you want the transition to occur.

Animating Elements

If you want to animate certain elements of a slide, you can follow the same process – just click on an individual element instead of the whole slide. Under this transitions window, clicking 'Add animation' will let you add the same effects to a single box. You can layer these by item and press 'Play' at the bottom to preview.

Above: Transitions can be added to help your presentation have a professional flow.

Above: Animations can be added to each component of a slide by selecting it.

MANAGING YOUR SLIDES

As you build up your presentation, managing your slides becomes important to ensuring your finished presentation is tidy and effective.

Deleting Slides

Decided a slide is unnecessary? Fine, delete it. You can do this by right-clicking the slide you want to lose and selecting 'Delete slide' from the pop-up list of options.

Reordering Slides

You can reorder slides simply by clicking and dragging them up and down the thumbnail list of preview slides. If you want to move a specific slide to the top or bottom of a long list, you can right-click it and select either 'Move slide to beginning' or 'Move slide to end'.

Numbering Slides

Although your slide thumbnails are numbered, the individual slides aren't. You can easily number them though. To do this, you'll need to select 'Slide numbers' under the 'Insert' menu and set them to 'On'. Now a number should show in the bottom-right corner of each slide.

Importing Slides

You can import slides from your existing presentations. To do this, you'll need to select 'Import' from the 'Insert' menu and manually select which slides from which presentations you want to add.

Above: Individual slides from previous presentations can be imported to your latest creation.

SHARING YOUR PRESENTATION

As with Docs and Sheets, Slides lets you share your work with friends, colleagues and, well, anyone who uses Google apps. You can let them view or edit your presentation, and share with individuals or groups. To send your presentation to someone, select 'Share' from the 'File' menu and enter the person's email address.

Collaborating on Presentations

If you want your recipients to be able to collaborate on your presentation with you, before pressing 'Send', you'll need to ensure the drop-down menu next to the contact box shows a pencil and reads 'Can edit'.

PRINTING YOUR PRESENTATION

You're not limited to sharing your presentation digitally; you have the ability to print out physical copies too. To do this, you will need to click the small printer icon (next to the 'Create new slide' button) and select how many copies you want to print.

Hot Tip

Want physical copies of your presentation to hand out at a meeting? You can fit multiple slides on a single page by selecting 'File' and clicking 'Print settings and preview'.

Above: When printing presentations through Slides, you can choose to have multiple slides per page.

ACCESSING SLIDES OFFLINE

Printing isn't the only way to access your presentation offline. If you've installed Google Drive on your machine, you can ensure your presentation is set up for offline syncing. This will download a hard copy to your machine. Any changes made offline will update in the cloud the next time you sign in and sync.

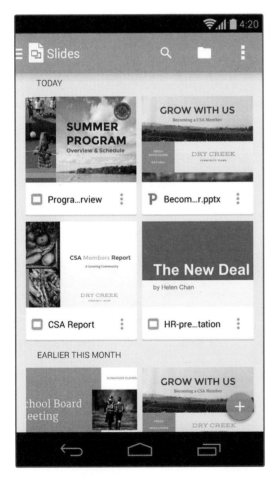

USING SLIDES ON MULTIPLE DEVICES

If you've left your laptop behind, you can use your smartphone or tablet to work on your presentations. Not only can you use your mobile device to update and edit your slides, the free iPhone and Android apps let you present on the small screen too.

Hot Tip

Sync Slides and Hangouts on your phone and you can present your presentation over a video call.

Left: Like Docs and Sheets, Slides has its own dedicated smartphone app.

CREATE A WEBSITE

As well as documents, spreadsheets and presentations, Google apps can be used to make your own website. This service for this is called Google Sites.

UNDERSTANDING GOOGLE SITES

Sites is a structured web page creation tool that lets you build up basic websites, piece by piece on a structured template. Giving you simple building blocks, it is designed to let teams collaborate easily, but can be shared with the wider internet too. Most importantly, you don't need to learn to code to create a website with Sites.

GETTING STARTED

Using Sites to create a web page is far less daunting than it sounds. Visiting sites.google.com and clicking the 'Create' button will get the process started.

CHOOSING A DESIGN

Sites is laid out in a very similar fashion to Google Slides. Instead of creating presentation slides, however, you're creating individual web pages that can be of varying length. You can pick your design from a selection of

Above: There are a number of pre-made designs available to help speed up the process.

themes. These are found in the right-hand menu under the 'Themes' tab.

ADDING CONTENT

Besides the 'Themes' tab is the 'Insert' tab. This lets you add content to your website. From text boxes to images and YouTube videos to Google Maps locations, there are special buttons that will help you add whatever you like.

Above: You can learn to create your own website using Google Sites.

Working with Google Apps

You can also add documents from other Google apps such as Docs and Sheets. Clicking these buttons lets you pick files from your Google Drive.

Above: To create a site, you'll need to choose what web address it is assigned to.

These are added to your website in fixed-size boxes that can be scrolled through.

Editing Content

Unhappy with what you've added? That's okay, it's not set in stone. Sites lets you go back and edit it as much as you like. To do this just click on one of your content boxes and press the trashcan icon that appears.

PUBLISHING YOUR SITE

See that big purple 'Publish' button at the top of the page? Yeah? Press that. This is the first step towards publishing your website on the internet, or internal company intranet. The next is entering the URL (website address) under which you want the page to sit.

Who Has Access to the Site?

This is completely down to you. During the publishing process, you'll be asked whether you want your site you be publicly visible or limited to internal company use. You can change this later in settings.

USING FORMS

The final Google app we're going to explore is Google Forms. Here you can create a means of collecting data for a variety of uses in a simple, speedy manner. Here is how to get started with Forms.

WHAT IS GOOGLE FORMS FOR?

With customized data-capture fields, you can use Google Forms to create surveys or polls, enter customer data, collect emails for a newsletter, or receive confirmation of who's coming to your party. You can leave your forms looking official and businesslike, or fill them with more personalized images and colours.

CREATING A FORM

Like with all other Google apps, you can create a new form either by selecting 'New' from your Google Drive homepage, or by pointing your browser at the dedicated holding page, in this case forms.google.com.

Blank Forms

To create a new blank form, select the big 'Blank' button on the Forms page. Now you need to decide on the purpose of your form. You can allow results to be entered in a variety of ways, including multiple-choice answers, check boxes, drop-down lists or time slots.

Above: Google Forms lets you create questionnaires and quizzes to gather information.

What's Your Form For?

This collection of input options makes Forms perfect for creating everything from quizzes to order forms. Try not to overcomplicate your form with too many entry options though.

Adding Queries

To add a query to your form, you simply click on the Questions tab and type your own question. If offering multiple-choice answers, you can do this by clicking on the answer fields.

Above: Forms can include queries, such as, 'Will you be attending this event?'

SENDING YOUR FORM

Once made, it's time to start getting some answers. You can send your form to desired recipients by clicking the large 'Send' button at the

Hot Tip

Need a specific piece of information? Mark questions as mandatory by selecting the 'Required' top of the page. You can choose whether to send it via email, link or by embedding it into an existing web page.

Sharing Your Form

If you want someone to help work on your form before it's shared with the masses, selecting 'Share' from the 'File' menu will help you do this. The usual sharing options of edit, view and comment are there to choose from.

Your Results

Thanks to its cloud nature, Forms will automatically pull all of your results into your files. Clicking on the 'Responses' tab of a completed and sent form will show you all of the current results.

Hot Tip

Get your Gmail contacts book at the ready as you can copy and paste contacts into the Form sending box to save you having to remember email addresses.

Above: You can send forms by entering the email addresses of desired recipients.

GO FURTHER

GETTING MORE OUT OF GOOGLE APPS

You've learnt the basics, so now it's time to look at some of the other features Google apps have to offer. Here we'll show you how to find solutions to your problems, join discussion groups and look at Google's own social network.

THE OTHER GOOGLE APPS

Docs, Sheets, Slides and Forms might be the most popular Google apps, but they're far from the only ones. There is a variety of apps, including ones that can help you track your entire organization's email (Vault), create a social presence (Google+) and host discussion groups.

Above: There is a whole range of Google apps besides Docs and Sheets.

USING GOOGLE VAULT

Google Vault is a service that lets you manage your entire organization's mail and Google Drive-stored files. Vault is exclusive to paying business customers and is included in the package that costs £6.60/$10 per user per month.

SIGNING UP TO GOOGLE VAULT

To sign up to Google Vault, you'll need to create a full G Suite account. You can do this by visiting gsuite.google.com/pricing and clicking the 'Get started' button of the Business package. To sign up, you'll need to provide banking details for a monthly direct debit.

THE BENEFITS OF GOOGLE VAULT

The main benefit of using Google Vault is peace of mind. It stores user data beyond standard retention periods and lets you recover lost information through eDiscovery – the process of

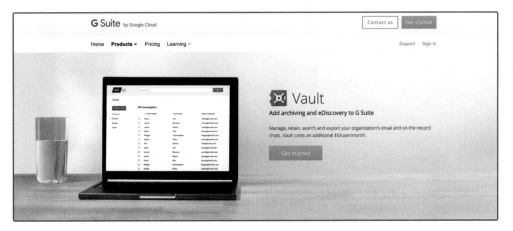

Above: Vault, a paid-for service, lets you back up an entire company's email.

seeking and finding information in electronic format. As well as helping with lost information, it can prove invaluable if you're ever faced with legal matters that require records to be provided.

USING GOOGLE VAULT

Once you've set up Google Vault it will run in the background uninterrupted. But first, you must tell it how long you wish to retain your company's information for, such as emails and on-the-record chats.

Setting the Timeframe

How cautious do you want to be? Vault lets you select from a variety of timeframes, or you can add your own. You can choose the number of days all the way up to 36,500. That's a staggering 100 years. Want more? You can ask it to store indefinitely; just remember to keep paying your bills.

Finding Information

If a legal situation occurs, you can use Vault's Google-powered search tool to quickly and securely retrieve information. Even if accounts have since been closed, their Vault-stored records will live on.

Above: Once set up, Vault will run uninterrupted in the background without prompting.

SETTING UP ON MULTIPLE DEVICES

The whole point of Vault is that it can track an entire company's actions. As such, Vault can be used to record data from all desired accounts within the firm. These can be selected by entering individual account details. An administrator will then be able to access all Vault files from any machine using their own special login.

Tracking Activity

Just to be on the safe side, you can track the activity of your Vault. A detailed audit of all searches, message views and exports are recorded to help protect both the privacy of employees and the safety of your company.

Above: Admins can keep track of Vault activity and run queries to see who has accessed what information.

GOOGLE'S OWN SOCIAL NETWORK

Facebook, Twitter and Instagram might be the world's most popular social networks, but they're not the only ones. Google has its own social network, bringing its users from across the world closer together with its service, Google+.

WHAT IS GOOGLE+?

Google+ is Google's very own social network. It lets users communicate with friends and colleagues across the world by adding them to their 'Circles'. It can also be used by businesses as a way to better communicate with staff and customers. You can post statements for all to see or have conversations with individual people.

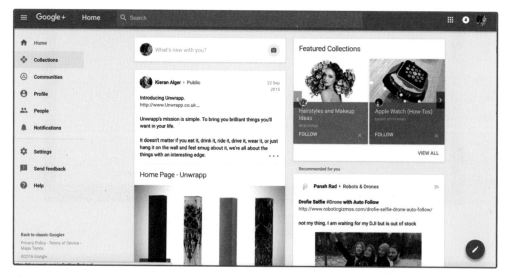

Above: Once signed up, you can start following people on Google+.

HOW DO YOU SIGN UP?

By creating a Google account, you've taken a significant step to signing up to Google+. Before your profile is publicly visible, however, you'll need to finish creating your profile. That involves confirming your birthday and adding a profile picture. That's it – you're set up.

USING GOOGLE+

Once your account's created, it's time to start adding content, seeing who else is out there and generally just being social. Not before you've customized your profile though, to make yourself stand out.

Above: Google+ lets you customize your own account, much like Facebook.

Your Profile

This is where all of your content will live. It's everything you post, share and comment on in one place. It's also what other people can see of you, so it's important it stands out. You can view your profile by clicking the 'Profile' tab on the left-hand menu run. Once in, a large 'Edit profile' button will let you customize your page.

Custom Edits

When editing your profile, you can add a profile picture, offer up certain information about yourself and add a themed header image. You can also choose what people can and can't see about you.

Posting Something

To post on Google+, you will need to click the large pencil symbol in the bottom-right corner of the page. Here you can write messages, add images and include links to content you want to share with people you know.

Seeing Others' Posts

To see other people's posts, first you must follow them. To do this, you'll need to visit the 'People' tab of the left-hand menu. Here you'll be recommended people based on those you

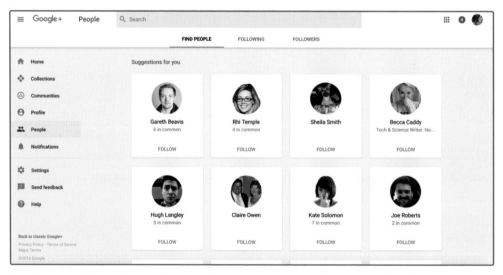

Above: You can search for people you may know or have Google make suggestions based on your email inbox and contacts.

already follow and whom you generally converse with through Google. You can also manually search for people by name.

Multi-Device Support

Like its more productivity-focused siblings, Google+ can be used on all manner of different devices. This is in addition to a browser-based platform that lets you access the social service on any internet-connected laptop or desktop.

Get the App

As well as being available on your traditional machines, dedicated Google+ mobile apps let you use the platform on your smartphone and tablet too. With these, you can keep on top of social actions whilst on the move. They can be found for free in the iOS App Store and Google Play Store.

Above: Items and articles can be shared on Google+ by clicking the logo.

Integrating Google+ into Your Apps

If you really want to share your Google apps creations with the world, you can post and share links to your docs, sheets, slides or forms on Google+. This is useful if you're looking to conduct a consumer survey, as you can share a custom form with all your followers.

Looking Out for the Logo

Google+ doesn't just let you post on its own page; it has share buttons dotted around the web. These offer one-click sharing when you're already signed in. Often found on news and retail websites, this button is a red icon with a letter 'g' and a '+' symbol.

GOOGLE GROUPS

Google Groups is a service that lets you hold online and email-based discussions without the faff or clutter of back-and-forth threads. You can use Groups to host discussions or make plans with teams, friendship groups or an entire organization.

GETTING STARTED WITH GROUPS

To start creating a Group, you'll need to log in to your Google account and direct your browser to groups.google.com. Here you'll be able to see groups you're already a member of or create a new one.

Above: You can manage all of your groups directly from one location.

Creating Groups

To create a new group, you'll need to click the large 'Create group' button at the top of the page. Before the group is ready for chats and discussions, however, you'll need to fill in a few details.

Above: You can create your own groups and discussion boards using Google Groups.

Filling Out the Form
First you'll need to name your group and give it a host URL and description. You can also select the sort of group you want to make, from a basic email list to a web forum, Q&A forum or collaborative inbox.

Privacy Settings
You also need to decide who can access the group. At the bottom of the set-up page, you'll need to choose who can join, view or post in the group. Each level of permission has a range of options, including invite-only and public.

Taking Charge
Once your group is created, you can assign managers or keep control of it yourself. Be warned though – depending on the level of access people have, this can become a busy job.

Posting in Groups
Once created, it's time to start posting in your groups. Unlike old-fashioned forums and

Google Groups	🔍
My groups	»
Starred topics	»
Recent items	
📁 **Recently viewed**	»
📁 **Recently posted to**	»
📁 **Recent searches**	»
johnson.luke88@gmail.com · Switch accounts · Desktop	

Above: Although there's no app, Google Groups has a mobile-friendly site.

message boards, this isn't a basic text-only offering. Rich text means you can change the font, colour and size of your posts. You can also add images.

Speedy Posting
As Google Groups plays nicely with keyboard shortcuts, such as Ctrl + V to paste, you can speed up your posts. You can see all the available shortcuts by pressing the '?' symbol.

Groups on the Move
Unlike Docs, Sheets and the others, a Groups mobile app isn't available. That doesn't mean you can't use it on the move though. A mobile-optimized site (groups.google.com/forum/m) makes messaging on the move a simple joy.

TROUBLESHOOTING

Here we'll look at common problems you might encounter while using Google apps, and how you can solve them. If the answer to your issue isn't here, you can find more answers at support.google.com.

MY FILES AREN'T SYNCING

Occasionally, when you update a document offline, it won't instantly sync when you reconnect to the internet. You can fix this and force the sync process by opening your Google

Drive tab. This should be stored in the top bar of your computer next to the Wi-Fi signal icon and battery life.

GOOGLE APPS IS SLOWING MY COMPUTER DOWN

Occasionally, using Google apps can cause your computer to slow down and stutter. More often than not, this is because you have too many tabs open in your browser. This can cause your computer to try to perform too many tasks simultaneously, slowing it down. Try shutting down some of your open tabs to speed things up.

FORGOTTEN PASSWORDS

If you've forgotten your password, you will need to visit Google's Account Support Page. Here you'll have to answer a number of security questions you set up when you created your account. Answer these correctly and Google will let you reset your password.

CALENDAR NOT SYNCING ON SMARTPHONE

A number of users have reported issues with calendar entries not syncing properly on the mobile Calendar apps. It sounds like an obvious solution, but Google's answer is to physically close the application and reopen it. All calendar entries should now appear on your phone.

HANGOUTS NOT APPEARING

Occasionally, in Gmail your Google Hangouts messages won't show and Hangouts contacts won't be visible. One way to fix this issue is to try refreshing your browser.

OUTDATED SOFTWARE

Not all features of your favourite Google apps will work if you're running old software. As Google apps run online, this means an out-of-date internet browser. If you're encountering problems, try updating your browser. The two most recent versions of Chrome, Firefox, Safari and Microsoft Edge are all supported.

ACCIDENTALLY DELETED FILES

If you've accidentally deleted a file from your Google Drive, don't worry – it can be recovered. In your Drive, click the 'Bin' tab on the left-hand menu. Once you've found your file in the bin, right-click it and press the 'Restore' option that pops up. It should now reappear in your Drive.

USEFUL WEBSITES AND FURTHER READING

WEBSITES

edutrainingcenter.withgoogle.com
Lessons for teachers on integrating Google tools into classroom settings.

www.gclearnfree.org/googledocuments
Tutorials on Google Drive and Docs, with links to other tutorials, such as on Sheets.

gsuite.google.com/learning-center
Interactive teaching service provided by Google for all apps and Google services.

www.lynda.com/Google-Apps-training-tutorials/1673-0.html
Online classes (paid/free trial) on Google Accounts, G Suite, Google Apps Script (GAS) and transitioning from Office to Google.

productforums.google.com
Forums exclusively for Google product assistance.

www.siteground.co.uk/tutorials/googleapps
Tutorials on Google apps, configuring app settings and domain ownership.

www.support.google.com
Google's help centre for any Google product, including all the G Suite apps.

FURTHER READING

Brumbaugh, Kyle and Musallam, Ramsey, *Creating a Google Apps Classroom: The Educator's Cookbook*, Shell Education Pub, 2014

Highfill, Lisa, and Hilton, Kelly and Landis, Sarah, *The HyperDoc Handbook: Digital Lesson Design Using Google Apps*, EdTechTeam, 2016

Khan, Saqib, *Mastering Google Drive and Docs*, CreateSpace Independent, 2013

Lamont, Ian, *Google Drive & Docs in 30 Minutes: The unofficial guide to the new Google Drive, Docs, Sheets & Slides*, i30 Media Corporation, 2015–2016

Procopio, Mike, *Instant Google Drive Starter*, Packt Publishing, 2013

Robinson, Noah, *Google Drive: The Ultimate Beginner's Guide to Mastering Google Drive*, 2016

Rutledge, Patrice-Anne and Gunter, Sherry Kinkoph, *My Google Apps*, Pearson Education, Inc., 2016

Teeter, Ryan and Barksdale, Karl, *Google Apps for Dummies*, Wiley Publishing, Inc., 2008

Wolff, Dominic, *Tame Your Gmail in 5 Easy Steps with David Allen's GTD*, Organized Living Press, 2014

Travis, Hunter, *Google Docs: The Unofficial Guide*, Minute Help Press, 2011

INDEX